THE GARDEN BEYOND

By K A Austin

Is there anything to be learned from a book?

Why yes dearest.

But the lessons

Are yours to glean.

The Garden Beyond

Published by ChristArt

Cover artwork ChristArt.co.uk

Cover design Freemanart.co.uk

To the Light of my life,

My Saviour and my King.

❦ *FOREWORD* ❧

"This is an absolute gem of a book! Kate's mastery of words and imagination, coupled with her walk with the Beloved, gives birth to stories of surprising encounter and wisdom.

Refreshingly written, it is a book of creative lightness that may be consumed at one sitting. Alternatively it may be used as a springboard for divine encounters, deepening our journey, and exploring the intertwining of God's love with our own spirituality of 'becoming' and 'being' sent to reflect His love."

Rev'd Tina C. Hodges

✄ *INTRODUCTION* ✄

The blindness of lies filled my soul. I dwelt in a dark garden of murky memory. Putrid vines wound their strangling network of depravation around my life. I searched in vain for a window of light.

Then a hand reached for me and I grasped it, unaware of the unseen power it contained, unaware of the God Who had ordained my accidental birth. I stood confused in the crowded centre of a cacophony of unfamiliar praise. A single voice rang out,

"Behold! I stand at the door and knock."

My inner being trembled, and there in depths imprisoned, I felt the echo of a firm and gentle knock.

"If anyone hears My voice and opens the door, I will come in…"

The voice, clear above the singing, persisted in its internal knocking.

Who is this that can reach the depths of my soul?

Silence.

I will answer.

The decision that changed my life forever.

And the door creaked slowly open on its hesitant hinges. The King stepped over the threshold and took His ordained place. Light exploded in my garden and darkness was expelled. Relief flowed in rivers down my cheeks. And Love cradled me in His eternal light.

❦ CONTENTS ❧

✎ *COMMISSION* ✎

We walked across dew-drenched fields up an incline, towards a seasoned oak standing guard over the waking world. A soft breeze blew gently through my hair, combing out the last dregs of sleep. He walked in determined strides and my instinct kept pace with Him. Leaning against the ancient tree, I studied Him. He stood upright, with a strong hand firmly grasping His shepherd's staff. The air around Him shimmered with light as He focused intently on the far horizon. Suddenly He turned, and His eyes penetrated to the heart of me, holding me in utter stillness.

"To be a servant in My footsteps is the highest calling."

I found myself lying in sea of waving grass, looking up at a clear blue sky. The swishing field brushed my outstretched arms as I stretched to reflect the silhouette of a large cross standing in silent solidity at my feet. As I lay there, the shadow of the cross moved slowly across my body and sank into me. Allowing its meaning to permeate, I marvelled at the intertwined depth and lightness of its weight. His hand lifted me to my feet. Removing His cloak, He wrapped it around me. The material brushed against my cheek and the scent of warm wool and something undefinably delicious enfolded me. Perseverance claimed me, and I stood, the cross within, the mantle without.

"Go forth."

His eyes returned to the far distance and I followed His gaze. The world held its breath and doors were opened. Thousands upon thousands of faces peered out. Young faces wearing hope. Old faces, worn and waiting. He walked among them in humble authority; I took a step and overflowed with the joy of being firstly His servant and secondly theirs.

"Be fruitful."

His gentle strength rested over my thumping heart, and I glimpsed through His eyes the fruit that had grown within me. I knew, as I followed Him, He would increase it.

"Multiply."

Our vision turned outward once more, and I saw us gathering the souls of the many waiting faces and as we gathered, we multiplied and became a great forest that covered the earth. And the earth was reborn, transformed into a garden of life with colours and creatures that danced into eternity.

"Subdue."

In my mind I saw streams of dark thoughts turn to rivers and snake into estuaries of inner struggle. I was flung this way and that, by feelings of self and pride, like a matchstick tossed in a stormy sea. I could not subdue my own mind; it conquered without mercy. He laid His hand upon my head and as Love wove its way through my senses, I yielded in relief to His touch. Light was born in every recess until my inner being was a network of glowing threads belonging to Him. Peace flooded me as realisation filtered through.

I see! All is subdued with Love.

The ancient oak remained steadfast on its deep roots.

I smiled up at Him, and His eyes shone back.

"I AM with you always."

~ TERRITORY ~

I trudged through thick mud, sticky and clinging to my boots. Intermittently I stomped, trying to remove some of the unwanted clod.

This part of the woods was dense, brambles knit together in a Sleeping Beauty hedge of impenetrable thorns.

Drat! I'll have to go all the way around.

A sigh deflated my lungs. My shoulders sagging, I set myself a dogged pace and clomped onward.

"Aha! Thank goodness!"

A welcome gap in the spikey resistance. Twigs snapped underfoot as I skipped through and turned to follow the grassy lane.

"Oh! Hello there!"

Somewhat startled, I addressed an unusually bold pheasant which had sprung out of nowhere and was now sprinting alongside me. A slither of uneasiness crept up the back of my neck, prickling my hair line.

Strange, pheasants aren't normally as confident...

The attack was so shocking and sudden that I shrieked. Flapping feathers and squawking beak came at me from all sides. I grabbed at a dried reed and thrashed the little beggar, but still he came on, wings buffeting, claws scratching, unrelenting in his territorial defence. I swished and swatted until the reed had disintegrated. The pheasant however remained undeterred. I bolted.

"Phew!"

Puffing and panting, I flopped onto the grass at the top of the track. The pheasant stayed at the bottom, strutting about in a very satisfied way, sporting his orange waistcoat and flashing his green tail feathers in triumphant victory.

"Love, what on earth was that all about?"

His chuckle surrounded me.

"I'm not sure I think it's so funny. That thing nearly incapacitated me!"

The chuckling got louder.

"Hrmph!"

"Creation can be very territorial. It is better to open your doors and allow such creatures to come to you. Intruding on them will only goad them to anger and resistance."

Now He tells me!

❧ *FEAR* ❧

How dark it is.

The midnight sky was moonless and the pin prick stars so far above that, if I stared straight at them, they disappeared. The cold night clasped at my jacket with icy fingers. My breath floated in foggy clouds that clung to my face as I walked.

"Love, what are we doing out here at this time of night?" I whispered, shivering.

I'm cold, the night is black and I want to curl up with a hot drink!

No answer.

Wrapping my arms around myself, I turned a corner and stopped dead! Before me was a large entity. A thick and dark mass; a heavy and dense presence. The acrid stench of fear oozed from it, freezing my eyes wide open. A strangled sound escaped my throat and feeling rushed through my legs, burning, searing: run, run, RUN!

I fled, the hard stone of the road thudding beneath my feet in time with the rush of blood thumping in my ears.

Some time later and still trembling, I tried to curl up with a hot drink.

"Love," I whimpered. "What was that? Where were You?"

Slowly, the golden light of His face overcame the darkness seeping into my heart.

"It was fear. I was where I always AM."

The cup in my hand slowly stopped shaking.

Breathe - just relax. He never left. There's a lesson in here somewhere.

I gave myself a sensible talking-to and went to bed.

Bolt upright, sticky with sweat, I fought my way out of the tangled covers and flicked on the lamp.

Memory of the dream returned in shattered patches…

I was on a bus. A rowdy crowd got on. The smell of alcohol stung my nostrils. Butterflies fluttered in my stomach. The pace of my breathing increased. I stared at my knees and tried to be invisible. The crowd was shouting and shoving each other aggressively. The driver protested and was silenced with a fist. I hugged myself to the window. My heart banged against my ribs. There were other people on the bus. One pretended not to see. Another hid in a hooded jacket. Someone grabbed my bag. My heart missed a beat. I looked up and down again. The pock-marked young man snarled at me.

I woke up.

Over the next few days, I played the dream over in my mind, with the addition of my own happily-ever-after ending. I became the saviour of the bus, and all were in awe of my swift martial-arts-like abilities. But inside I cringed with shame as fear's black eyes hovered hauntingly in the background.

It was a few days before I was able to summon enough courage to approach the subject.

"Love, what's going on? Why am I so afraid?"

"Fear is not just a feeling; it is a strategic enemy with a purpose. It seeks to disable you by infiltration."

Well, it's doing a pretty good job.

"I AM the King of creation, and nothing happens without My Word. I AM Love, and all I will for you is good. Trust in My Love, and fear will flee from you."

I thought of the times I had trusted His love for me, even when I didn't understand, even when it hurt. There was peace in that place of trust. In contrast, I remembered times I had not trusted and stress and fear had reigned.

"And more than that, if you love them..."

Images from the dream rushed back and anger clamoured to defend the fear.

I don't want to love them; I want You to sort them out!

I cut Him off with a thought and sulked until I could bear it no longer.

"You want me to love those thugs when what I really want to do is give them a taste of their own medicine," I blurted in a hoity-toity high tight squeak.

"I understand what it is to be intimidated, to be beaten, and yes, even killed, and yet..."

Gently Love's presence filled my sight. The scars He wore were bound to Him by actions not only committed by those on the bus. I saw the cuts He bore for me. He loved me, without reservation. How then could I refuse? The walls of resistance began to crumble.

"I'm sorry; it's just that I've been bullied so many times I don't know if I really want to love them, even to please You...," my voice shrank into nothing.

Slowly my eyes were opened and I saw the 'thug' from the bus. His eyes wore the defence of violent anger, but behind it, I saw the fear. It was fear that drove him! As I watched amazed, he shrank into a child. A man held him against the wall by his throat and shook him. The sound of small teeth rattling buzzed in my head. The man dropped him and snatching up a bottle filled with despair disappeared into another room. The door of compassion opened in my heart. I saw the 'thug' with understanding. I saw the man with pity.

"You see, they are all loved by Me. They are damaged and so they damage others. Look at 'why' rather than 'what'. Choose to love and you will be free of fear."

My heart submitted to His wisdom. Holy love swept through me like a fresh wind, and I was liberated.

❧ *FISHING* ❧

Why is fishing so boring?

I had been standing for hours without a single
bite, not even a tickle. I had tried everything,
from throwing food out onto the water, to tempt
the fish to reveal themselves, to chucking rocks at
the reeds to wake any sleepers.

But nothing!

Perhaps there just aren't any fish here.

I hummed dolefully to myself, staring at a
kingfisher clad in royal blue, perched on a willow,
turning his head this way and that as if listening
for the fish.

A pair of crows cawed their raucous racket above me. I looked up, frowning, into the loving face of the Son.

"Oh! I didn't hear You arrive." I jumped, startled.

"No, you didn't." His eyebrow arched.

He gets that from His Father.

"Can you help? I'm having trouble catching these slippery little articles!" I asked, a slight whine in my tone.

Where has He been while I've been wasting my time here catching nothing!

His silence arrested me.

"I've tried everything I can think of," I said quietly.

My mind glanced back through the last few hours. The endless waiting and watching. Fruitless time wasted that I could never get back. The emotions that had surged within me, ranging from eager anticipation to frustrated desperation.

"They just don't seem to want to take the bait." I slumped defeated onto the grass.

He stood tall and looked out across the lake. A faint glow radiated from Him, softening my sass. A light breeze picked up, rippling the surface and tousling my ruffled hair.

"Perhaps you'd like to try it My Way." A patient smile creased the corners of His eyes.

I sighed despondently. I'd had enough really, but one more go wouldn't hurt. I warmed myself with His presence and nodded. He bent and retrieved the rod, holding me with His gaze.

"There are many ways to catch fish, but only one way is truly effective."

I sat up straight. The reel sang as He wound it in, His fingers flying over the mechanism with precision. I watched as He flicked the line out of the water, showering us both with cold droplets.

"Firstly, the right food."

He took something from His pocket and fixed it carefully to the hook. I squinted trying to see what it was.

"Secondly, the right place."

He turned slightly so that His direction altered and He was facing the far right of the lake, where the kingfisher had been. I breathed deeply the cool clear air and tentatively touched the hem of His robe.

"Thirdly, the right time."

He leaned back and swung the rod. I followed the line flying through the air, its perfect curve slowly releasing into a far-reaching cast. I heard the tiny splosh as the weight disappeared into the lake, and the line settled for a second on the surface before it was swallowed.

I stood up beside Him, holding my breath. He looked at me, His eyes full of an eternity of fishing for men. He handed me the rod, and almost immediately I felt the welcome tug of a catch. His scarred hand closed over mine, and together we wound in the reel.

My mind flickered back. I was in a classroom telling a group of young children my story. When I was asked to take this particular class, I had searched for His guidance on how to show them Who He was. I remembered the clarity of His words.

"Gently and simply does it; just tell the story and I will do the rest. All the while you are at work on the surface, I AM at work in the depths."

Revelation lit up the air around me.

The line flew out of the water, flashing with silver as it sailed towards us and landed with a soft thump on the grass at our feet. A gleaming fish lay dazzling in the sunlight. I gave a little clap and a chirrup.

"At last! Oh thank you, thank you!" His hand cupped my chin and lifted my eyes to His.

"Everyone is different as is every circumstance, and so one formula for all does not work. Instead, cultivate an ear that hears Me, and in listening, you will be in the right place at the right time, with the right tools."

❧ *ABANDONED* ❧

A brood of ducklings paddled by in arrow formation, like fat, scruffy bumble bees. We stood comfortably against the railings that separated us from the bubbling stream. The bright rays of a spring-day sun beat down, warming the top of my head.

"This is lovely?" I announced, the hint of a question in my statement.

"Just watch," He breathed over me, still looking at the fluffy babies.

They had landed and were stumbling up the muddy bank, darting about and foraging for food among the sparse reeds and grass. Finding nothing, they stood and intermittently held up their little beaks to the wind. The series of shrill cheeps that burst forth would summon any mother's heart from the four corners of the earth.

I chuckled with delight.

He laid His arm around my shoulder, and I settled into Him. A feeling of complete safety washed over me. I breathed a great sigh and leaned heavily. We waited. No mother duck came. The ducklings staggered about, their cries rising to a crescendo. I looked up at Him with a creased brow.

"Where is she?" I whispered, suddenly afraid.

He remained still. We waited. Still no mother duck came. The tiny babies slowed, their tired legs giving way. Scrunching themselves into little balls of brown and yellow fluff, their heads drooped and their eyes closed. My stomach rose in my throat; my eyes stung with tears that threatened to overflow.

"She's not coming, is she?" I gasped at Him, pulling away.

"She cannot."

Tears wove a stream down my cheeks, and my heart heaved in my chest.

"What can we do? We have to help them!" I pleaded frantically.

He held me in painful compassion until my tears were empty.

"You see that one?" He nodded towards a single duckling that was sitting at the edge, hopelessly staring into the water.

"Feed him."

"What about the others?"

"I didn't ask you to feed them."

"What will happen to them?"

He looked at me with such love. There was a deeper message; I could feel it, stirring just out of reach.

"What are you showing me, Love?"

I was thrust into chaos. A thousand exotic smells mingled with the odour of rotting rubbish assailed my nostrils. Buzzing insects and barking dogs competed with the cries of vendors calling out their wares. Multi-coloured silks fluttered gracefully atop market stalls that butted against one another like sardines in a can. Humidity coated me instantly in perspiration. A crowd of half-clothed, half-starved, sun-scorched children skittered past, their eyes wide and shifty and their shoulders hunched over. One of them looked up at me, pleading, with deep hollow eyes. I took a step back. I felt the hand of Love firmly in the small of my back, pushing me forward.

"What do you want me to do?" I stared at the gaunt child.

"Feed him."

There are hundreds of kids here. Is He going to ask me to feed them all?

"No, just this one."

And then I was watching scruffy ducklings asleep in the grass.

"Who were all those children?" I asked with a trembling heart.

"They are those that have been abandoned by the world."

I choked on His words.

Quivering and gasping inside, I asked,

"What can I do?"

"Feed him." He repeated.

"But what about the others?"

You can't just leave them there.

"There are many workers in My Father's Garden, and if everyone does what they can, it will be enough."

He turned to the ducklings, and I noticed a single tear on His cheek.

"Even though your father and mother forsake you, I will never leave you."

❧ *FAITH* ☙

The sheep bleated their morning songs to one
another as we walked quietly, side by side,
together but not touching. The pungent scent of
droppings and dew-soaked meadow drifted
around us. The grass grew soft and green beneath
our feet, creating a royal carpet that sank gently
with every step and sprang back behind us.
Pockets of silver-laced blades twinkled with last
night's chill in small dips alongside our path.

How contented I feel beside Him. How safe He is.

He led me to a tall and stately tree growing
unhindered, next to a pond whose waters lay
calm and glass-like.

"What do you see?" He gazed at me expectantly, and my heart swelled with wonder-filled love.

"I see You," I mumbled, almost speechless.

"Yes," He smiled and directed my face to the tree. **"And?"**

Oh, He wants me to look at the tree.

The tree, with its branches spreading majestically over the water and the meadow. Looking down at the pond, a perfect mirrored reflection stood as clear and stately as its owner, even to the colour and form of individual leaves.

A coldness reached my fingers, and I clutched the round, frosted-kissed pebble He had placed in my hand.

Splosh! There was an eruption of drops where it landed, and ripples in waves cascaded out from its inverted volcanic event.

The mirrored tree was shaken into oblivion for a moment, confirming its existence as just a reflection, before wobbling back into focus.

"I see the tree, and I see the reflection of the tree."

I knew by now that everything meant something.

"What are You asking me to see, Love?"

"This tree is called Faith and its reflection, Belief."

Looking back I recalled a time when I had listened to all those who knew more than I, and I had believed them. I remembered the things I had told myself were real because I had wanted them to be. I relived the moment when all that was not true faith had been stripped away through my own walk with pain, and I had seen how naked I was without Him.

I took a deep and steadying breath.

Light dawned, and I saw the moment true faith was born within me, and all the well-meant words and folly of my own making melted like ice in the sun.

His warm, strong hands rested on my shoulders.

"Faith is to the spirit as the beating heart is to the body. And there it matures.

Belief is to the spirit as clothing is to the body. It can be changed or taken off.

Faith comes from Me. Belief comes from you."

✺ *FAMILY* ❧

Crouched beneath the spikey hawthorn, I sensed Him beside me, comfortingly un-prickly. Twilight played its music of goodnight birdsong to the deepening shadows. I could almost taste the rising scent of damp leaves all around as the heat of the day withdrew. Five young badgers romped on the grass, emitting little grunts with every bombarding fluffy roll. I searched for His hand and squeezed it with delight. He turned slightly and the comfort of His mantle settled over me. We watched the tumbling cubs snuffle in the dust, regularly bobbing their striped noses upwards to sniff the evening smells. One scratched at a patch of earth, uncovering a desired delicacy. Instantly another snapped at it, resulting in a flurry of fighting. With bared teeth and growling, they shoved their furry bodies into each other in an attempt to win the prize. A large and sleep-drunk boar emerged from the entrance to the sett. Cuffing the nearest cub and biting the rump of another, he claimed his breakfast. A red patch seeped slowly across the back of the bitten cub. He scratched at it, whimpering helplessly.

Oh Love.

 Gasping, I started to rise, but His hand weighed heavily upon me, and I could not move.

"Watch."

With a pounding heart, I leaned eagerly forward. The young cub waddled away in widening circles, his whimpers fading.

"He's hurt! Please?"

I clasped and unclasped my hands urgently, rocking to and fro on my knees. His mantle slipped from my shoulders.

The head of a small sow came into view. She ambled into the clearing and nudged and fawned over the cubs one by one as they gathered around her. Lifting her head, she sniffed the air this way and that, searching out the missing offspring. She found him cowering under an elder bush. Using her snout, she gently but firmly pushed and shoved until he succumbed to her persuasion and she was able to lead him home.

I shifted uncomfortably, wondering at these animals and their capacity to both harm and help.

My own family flowed across my vision like moving photographs. Walking in the local woods, climbing trees and den building. Each of us full of our own happiness at being together. A different scenario followed. Shouting and fighting, siblings wanting their own way and neither prepared to compromise. I entered, shouting louder than any, brittle with tiredness and frustration.

I shrank into myself, cringing shamefully at my exposure.

"I'm not the best parent, am I, Love?"

"At times yes, at others, no."

"Help me!"

He lifted the fallen mantle and wrapped it gently but firmly around me.

"Your family are a gift and a lesson. If your love for them overcomes your self-love, there they will blossom and you will grow."

This was a truth that was hard to bear, but even my own heart was on His side, and so as usual, He won.

❧ *REST* ❧

We stood on a hillock dotted with tiny white flowers, like confetti.

"Come." His voice challenged my wandering thoughts. Clasping His offered hand, I dragged myself alongside Him through the grass.

Why am I so tired?

I cast my mind back over the last few days. We had worked, yes, but the work was not hard. Beside Him, working was an ease and a joy. So why was I tired?

I stole a glance, hoping to read an answer in His face. He was ready for me, as always. His eyes, a deep pool of all-knowing, swept through my spirit, and I had my answer.

"Your spirit is eternal and grows in strength in My presence, but your flesh is a temporary house which needs rest."

He walked slowly into a field of waving barley, its blades reflecting His light as they flowed with the breeze like a haze of silken hair. I followed, my hands brushing over the softly whiskered tops. I breathed deeply the rich smell of good earth and ripening crops. The sun's rays rested on the back of my bare neck, relaxing my shoulders into my arms and making my fingers feel fat and heavy. He turned, and wrapping me in light, He laid me down to rest. The steady drum of His heartbeat slowed my own as I lay my head against Him and drifted into a sleep of perfect peace.

The bright song of blackbirds brought me back to consciousness. I stared up at the pale blue of the sky with its wisps of fluffy white clouds puffing slowly across. The world felt new and vibrant. I looked up at Him Whom my heart loves.

"I love to watch you rest," His smile shone brightly on my face.

ॡ

ᴕ SACRIFICE ᴔ

The next morning, I sat watching the dawn creep up the horizon, bathing the waking world in fresh yellow light. I had heard the call of Love early this morning.

I wonder...

There He was, waiting by the open gate, His stance eager, almost leaning into the walk we had yet to begin.

"Ready?" Something in His tone alerted me.

"I'm not sure, ready for what?"

He raised an eyebrow at my momentary panic and held out a hand, igniting my trust.

We marched up the path, climbed over the stile, and set off across the open parkland. The wet grass soaked into my boots, darkening their sage green to emerald. A couple of uninterested horses grazed steadily, the sound of tearing pasture fading as we passed. Among the intermittent trees flowed the melody of the dawn chorus. We walked for some time, He, alive with the beauty of glory, me, content to be with Him.

He stopped at the closed gate. 'BEWARE OF THE BULL' glared at us in blood-red writing. I peered over apprehensively and He, putting His hand to the latch, looked at me with purpose. The gate clicked as He swung it wide open.

Oh great! I'm gonna be gored by a bull!

"Sacrifice is not always about dying; sometimes it is about living."

He walked boldly forward. My feet had grown roots and would not move.

"Help. I'm stuck!"

"As long as you stay with Me, all will be well."

All the moisture in my mouth seemed to evaporate, and I struggled to detach my lips from each other.

Yes, but Your idea of well isn't always the same as mine.

"I AM well, yes?" It wasn't really a question.

"And yet I made the ultimate sacrifice."

His eyes poured love that washed over and through me like molten courage. My lungs were suddenly released, and taking huge gulps of air, I stepped up to stand by His side. We followed the flattened grass into the open field. I scanned it intently, but there was no bull! He chuckled softly.

"Sacrifice is not always where you expect it to be."

Well, that's a relief, I think.

A little way down the path He stopped. I followed His eyes. There just under my next footstep was a large slimy worm.

Yuk, I nearly trod on it.

I stepped over it. He stood in expectant stillness. I looked back. He was looking at the worm. I looked at the worm.

Surely not, it's just a worm.

I knew by His face what it was He wanted. I was supposed to pick up the wriggling, slime-coated creation, and relocate it to a safer place.

Might as well get it over with; there'll be no moving Him until it's done.

It was cold to my touch. My senses recoiled at the ooze that spread across my fingers. I positioned the worm none too gently on a patch of bare earth a little way from the perilous path. Wiping my hands on the dewy grass, I linked my arm in His. He gave it a little squeeze. I glowed.

"Whatever you do for one of these little ones, you do for Me."

Aha, this is not just about worms. Goodness, I am slow sometimes!

He took off walking, at a faster pace. I trotted along to catch up, feeling like I was about three years old. A tiny, scruffy ball of feathers scooted across the path a few feet in front.

I stooped to gather it up into my hands.

"Leave it," His firm voice cut me to the heart.

"I can't just leave it. It's so small, it will be eaten or trodden on or..."

"Leave it," Firm and strong came the voice again.

Perhaps I misheard.

I looked at Him hopefully, but no, He had spoken, and of course, He always knows best.

I shut my eyes to the tiny bird with its beak opening and closing in a plea for nourishment. Wrenching myself away, I followed more slowly, my head hanging so low my chin almost touched my chest.

Suddenly He pulled me down off the path.

"Watch," He whispered.

I watched in wonder as an adult bird fluttered to the baby and coaxed it into a clump of nettles.

"Thank goodness!" I exclaimed, much relieved.

"Yes," He said with complete understanding.

"Sacrifice can sometimes mean withholding the thing you long to give."

I was right; it wasn't just about worms!

✖ *BALANCE* ✖

"Love, this bridge doesn't look safe!" I aimed my voice at Him carefully.

"Are you stalling?"

Stalling! I don't want to fall off into...

I looked over the side at the wet marsh. A stagnant waft hit me full in the nostrils.

"Pheeuww!"

"The quicker you cross, the quicker we will be on our Way."

Honestly! Sometimes I wonder exactly which way that is.

We had spent all day travelling. I was tired of it and grumpy. And as far as I could tell, we had done nothing constructive, nothing that was any use to anyone. Goodness, I really was grumpy!

I wobbled across the bridge, holding white-knuckled to the sides.

"Stop there," He called.

"I'm only half way," I replied as loudly as I dared, in fear of my voice somehow tipping the balance.

"Feel the movement."

Not now, please let me get off this stupid bridge first.

"The sooner you feel it, the sooner you can cross."

Stop listening to my thoughts!

His warm chuckle reached me, and I stifled a giggle.

I squeezed my hands around the rails and concentrated. Every time I moved, the bridge would counter my movement and shake precariously. Gradually my sense of balance began to move with the bridge.

"Now cross over," He called.

"On my way," I muttered.

The bridge and I became as one, and with each step we rocked back and forth in a fluid dance of shifting weight.

Once across, I sat beside Him on the grass. Light rain, like mist, began to fall. My brow crinkled, and I looked to Him for understanding.

"The whole of creation is made with balance at its core. For every thought, every action, there will be complete balance. Father is totally fair."

I clutched at the cold grass poking up between my fingers. Recollections of my own unpleasant nature rose to the surface of my mind. I was suddenly frozen with fear at the implications of the balance of my own actions. My eyes pleaded with Him for mercy.

"I have balanced all with My sacrifice." His eyes brimmed with understanding.

Gratitude flooded me like a bursting dam.

Thank you, thank you, thank you.

❦ DISINFECTANT ❧

On the windowsill was a small bottle of dark-blue glass embossed with golden writing. I peered at the blurred words. Remembering the glasses perched on my head, I adjusted them and looked again. It read, **'Heaven's disinfectant'.**

What on earth is heaven's disinfectant? I pondered, turning the bottle in my hands.

Slowly, His presence filled the room. The bottle glowed. I stilled.

"Upstairs," He breathed and His fragrance whirled around me.

"On my way," I responded, shrugging His mantle into place.

The moon shone a single ray of silver light onto the landing carpet. Intermittent scratching came from behind a closed door. I turned the knob and followed the path of moonlight as it entered the room of a sleeping child. To my disgust, it highlighted a large scab-encrusted rat scratching at the far end of the bed. The child moaned. I gasped and stepped back, pulling His mantle tighter.

"Yuk! There's a rat! What do I do?"

"Open the heavens," came the quiet, commanding voice, and I felt the cool glass bottle pulsate in my hand.

I moved cautiously forward, the rat eyed me intently, as it crouched, preparing to pounce. Holding out heaven's disinfectant with shaking hands, I unscrewed the lid. Golden ethereal mist rose from the opening, and with it came the soft sound of singing. Gradually the music built into a chorus of a thousand angels crying out in exaltation. Adoration rose higher until my spirit soared and I sang with all that was within me. The pure beauty of the music of heaven wove tear trails down my cheeks. The rat squealed and shrivelled into smoke, making a swift exit through a gap in the window frame. The child sighed softly and curled into a deep and natural sleep. I replaced the lid of my treasure and quietly closed the door.

Later that day I sought Him. "What is heaven's disinfectant, Love?"

His glory lit my face, filling my heart until I overflowed.

"My Spirit inhabits true worship, and before Me, no unclean thing can stand."

JIGSAWS

The scent of wisteria drifted through the open window with the afternoon breeze. I inhaled a sweet scented lungful and looked up from my book. Something new lay on the table, something that had not been there before. It was a piece of jigsaw the size of a dinner plate. As I picked it up and peered at it, an image began to materialise. A hand, flexing intermittently in what seemed to be an attempt to escape its captivity. There was someone trapped within the puzzle.

"Oh!" I dropped it onto the carpet.

"Bring it," the voice of the King, gently and firmly drew me.

Slipping the jigsaw piece under my arm, I went out. Winding my way in and out of trees and bushes, I entered the Garden. Rays of shimmering light filtered through branches as my feet trod the moss-covered path. Bees hummed alongside me, bobbing in and out of pollen laden blooms. The melody of a multitude of birds flew up and over the tree tops in an ever-flowing symphony. I was near Him; the sense of His nearness increased with every step. The puzzle shifted, almost writhed. I held it fast, and my heart trembled, echoing its unease.

A fellow pilgrim joined me. We shared a smile and, I noticed, a piece of jigsaw. We walked together in comfortable companionship for a time; then the paths separated and I walked on. The pull of the King's presence grew stronger. The piece of puzzle under my arm clenched. The hand moved to and fro across the surface, pushing, banging, and trying to get out.

I sped up, moving past the rippled water of the lake and through the shaded woodland glen with its heady wild honeysuckle. I stepped out into a circle of sentinel beeches, all bowing inwards. And there He was, in the centre, the King of Love in all His magnificence, shining brighter than the sun. The light of His countenance smiled at me and my eyes lowered. On the grass before Him was an almost completed puzzle. The image was a woman, her frantic face pleading from behind her transparent prison.

"What do You want me to do?" I bowed before His majesty.

"Play your part," His voice pulled me towards an empty space.

I lay my piece there. A perfect fit. Behind me waited the pilgrim I had shared a smile with on the journey. I stepped back. He placed his piece in the last gap and the picture was complete. She was on her knees now, her face buried in her hands softly sobbing. The King of Love drew near. Reaching into the image, He took her by the hand and lifted her out. Turning her face to His, He led her in the dance; twirling and laughing, He swept her off her feet. Her face shone with the reflection of His love. He poured grace and mercy until she was surrounded by only Him, and He was satisfied with the saving.

Then began the song. Such longing and wonder flowed out from the whole of creation that tears fell freely from all eyes. A golden song of Love fulfilled held the world in its embrace, while we danced with rapturous joy.

That evening, when all was quiet, I gave vent to gratitude.

"Oh Lover of souls, thank you for letting me share in the most amazing and best times."

His great heart pounded in my ears.

"For every one lost that is found, there is such joy in heaven it cannot be contained on earth."

✤ *FENCES* ✤

I love the early mornings. The birds with their wake-up songs, the scent of dew-spangled grass, and the way the rays shine through the leaves, making everything glow with a brighter shade of green. I stretched myself out on the garden chaise and thought of Him.

A large bird settled on the fence and eyed me suspiciously.

"Hello, you handsome creature."

I noted the dusky peach colour of its neck melting into a rich blue breast and folded wings which flickered with iridescence.

Wow, that's some bird!

"Beautiful, yes, on the outside."

I considered Him and lost myself in His kind of beauty that outshone all the birds in all the world.

"Look."

I followed His moving eyes and saw another arrival join the bird on the fence. This one was small and a shabby brown, although it did have attractive beady eyes that darted to and fro, as though it were searching for something specific.

"How sweet, if a little plain."

As I watched, yet another bird joined the growing company of assorted fence-perchers. Dainty and cheerfully bright yellow, with a crest that looked like a Robin Hood cap.

"Delightful!"

I leaned against Him and together we watched several more birds join the flock on the fence.

"What do you make of it?" He quizzed.

Uh oh, there's more to this than just a bunch o' birds sitting on a fence!

Behind the birds was the open sky and a wide expanse of scrub-land. In front of them was our garden, full of life and fruit and Him.

"They are sitting on the fence," I murmured quietly, my understanding growing.

"Yes."

"Can we invite them into our garden?"

"Yes."

He wasn't giving much away today!

"Will they come?"

"Maybe."

"How can we make sure they do?"

"Your part is to reveal Whom to call on in the day of trouble. The rest is up to them. You are not responsible for their choice."

That doesn't stop me wanting them all to come in.

"You are right in that it doesn't stop Love from desiring them, but Love never forces."

⊰ *TIME* ⊱

The grand house stood looking down on all its kingdom. Ornate windows cast their sight over the regal symmetry of trees lining the gravel drive. Pillars of ivory marble held up the stately and intimidating entrance. He grasped my hand and, ignoring the imposing architecture, led me firmly away.

"This way."

We walked to the outskirts of the grounds with their finely manicured lawns and perfumed beds until we came to the orangery, a long, glassed structure with the clear blue of the sky reflected in its panes. As we passed through the doors, the delicious aroma of warm lemons engulfed my senses. Drips of hot moisture fell in tiny splats on my head from the overcrowded foliage above us.

"Hmmm." He took a deep breath.

I studied His face, the light that radiated from it and the depths of unfathomable love in His eyes.

He is everything to me.

His smiled on me with kindness. Waving His arm over the growth of the tropical enclosure, He began.

"You see these trees with their fruit ready for picking, and these others with no fruit as yet?"

"Yes," I responded eagerly to His words.

"Each fruit matures in its own perfect time. Be consistently patient in your nurture. Do not hurry the process or you will cause damage. Some fruits can take years."

I thought of a particular friend I had known for a long time. She carried such heartache, and I longed for her to know His love. I loved her and she knew it. He loved her, but she knew it not. I remembered the many conversations we had shared about Him, but she had not entered into His embrace.

"Some fruits can take years."

His words gently embraced my thoughts. Sadness eased from my shoulders, and I stood taller.

"Yes, her time will come."

My heart jumped with anticipated joy. I took off, skipping through the open doors and over the fresh green grass. His laughter followed behind me while I twirled among the roses, slowing as excitement settled into a profound and trusting peace.

✧ *HIDDEN* ✧

Divine ambience shimmered through the living translucent pink walls that enclosed us, like the sun through rose petals. His hand opened before me, and with expectant interest I looked into His palm. A variety of seeds of different shapes, colours and sizes lay like babes in blankets. He chose a rich brown one, perfectly oval in form, and held it up to the light. My eyes were drawn into its centre, and a world of unseen universes was revealed. Spinning galaxies of colours without names and stars that sparkled like diamonds. And deeper still, the tiny seed's inner world beat with a sleeping heart.

"Wow!" I gasped in utter amazement.

I pulled myself back and met His gaze. In His eyes I saw the same life in such measure that my imagination stretched like an elastic cord until it reached the point of almost snapping. He paused to allow the cord to sit a moment, and then, He stretched it a fraction further, and I knew this was beyond me.

"I AM the power of creation."

The world I knew exploded into a million fragments of small-mindedness. I stood helpless before Him, my body hanging in timeless space and my mind expanding with the knowledge which exceeds imagination. Love lay a steadying hand on me. My pulse returned to its normal rhythm and my breath came back in gasps.

"When a seed is created, the power of creation is placed within. Then, when the time is just right..."

He breathed slowly over the seed pod, saturating it. The life within burst into a flash of glowing fire; its heart-beat pounding like an eager drum. Swirls of coloured light were released with a fragrance so sweet my eyes shed tears of excruciating joy. I found myself flexing the tingling numbness from my fingers and toes. He sat silently beside me, waiting for my return to verbalisation.

"Wow!"

"Exactly!" He stated matter-of-factly.

⤳ *UNDOING* ⤲

I sat on a familiar bench in the centre of our Garden, His presence permeating my heart with a sense of completeness.

How I love Him. How I love to be with Him.

A group of rabbits caught my attention, as their white tails bobbed about on the grass. One of them bounced over and sat at my feet, looking up expectantly. Sometimes I would bring them fresh fruits and vegetables and they would sit munching contentedly while I stroked them and cleaned their eyes. But not today, today I just wanted to be with Him without any other purpose or distraction.

I focused my heart and Holy fire blazed around me, soaking into my skin and connecting with the flame within. I leaned back and melted into the joy that filled my spirit.

How wonderful!

The rabbit at my feet nudged my shin with a soft nose, demanding attention. I moved my foot and gently but firmly pushed him away.

"Not now."

The rabbit was insistent, and in its determination enticed several other furry siblings to harass me. I was prodded and pushed in all directions.

"Love, can't you occupy them for a while, so that I can spend some time with You?" I exclaimed, tutting loudly.

I got up and moved away, hoping to rid myself of the little irritations. Thinking I had eluded them, I lay down on the grass. They followed! With bunnies bouncing all over me, my frustration reared its ugly head.

"For goodness sake, go away and leave me alone!" I almost shouted.

Undeterred, they jumped about in gleeful anticipation of some green delicacy I might have stuffed into a pocket somewhere. I gave up and left.

When the day was finally over, and I still had not managed to enjoy my time alone with Him, I lay in bed and grumbled.

"Spending time with You is impossible with continual interruptions. I am sorry but really You will have to do something about those rabbits if You want me to spend quality time with You."

Blah blah blah blah.

I was beginning to bore myself. He, however, waited patiently for my moan to end.

"I want you to take care of those small creatures."

"I do, but what about my time with You?"

Sacred stillness filled the room like the air before a thunderstorm.

"It's important to me. I need You," I whispered.

"Why?"

I don't understand.

My brain tumbled over itself in an attempt to decipher His meaning.

"Your desire is for yourself."

My defences crept up and tumbled. He was right. He was always right. My desire for time with Him was for myself. Disappointment sank into my soul. I curled into a ball and hid my face.

Love waited, then slowly compelled my focus. His eyes were filled with tears of compassion.

"I AM not turning you away, I AM taking you deeper. Your sacrifice must be total, even unto your sacrifice of Me."

"I am sorry, Love. I am so full of self; how can I ever be free?"

"With Me all things are possible."

Thank God.

❧ *MAN TRAPS* ❧

I looked into the cage at my feet. A small animal lay quietly in one corner, as though it had given up the fight to escape.

"Love?" I queried with my tone.

"Open the cage door," He commanded quietly.

I knelt and spoke gently to the creature as I lifted the catch and held open the door. A small unconcerned furry face stared into mine fleetingly before resuming its passive position.

"Come on. Silly thing. The door's open. You can come out."

I pulled a confused face. Love sighed sadly and carefully reached in, lifted the animal and set it down on the grass outside the cage. It stood, shook itself and ambled off into the bushes.

I don't get it.

"There are many traps that can seem right."

Aha.

Light began to dawn.

"In our search for You, we are sometimes trapped very comfortably without even realising it?" I questioned.

He looked grave and answered in a tone of voice that made me quake inside.

"It is hardest to reach those who believe they have already found what they seek. Those who have been converted by the schemes of man, however well meaning, have not found truth. The only true conversion comes by impartation from Father. If conversion is not true, when pain and hardship strike, the soul will collapse beneath the weight with nothing to sustain it, and the souls hope will be crushed. Then, no longer believing there is any worthiness in the pursuit of truth, it will give up seeking Me."

I fell prostrate with fear. My heart beating with trepidation. I asked in a trembling voice:

"How can we know it is really You we follow and not something else?"

"The real truth is unconditional Love."

✵ GOD PARTICLE ✵

I whooshed through the trees, leaves the colours of fire swirled about me like flitting embers. Sucking in the crispness of a golden autumn day, I leaned back against the trunk of a young sycamore wearing a coat of dull ivy leaves.

Time for a little self-reflection, I think.

My feet instantly felt restricted, and looking down I saw the ivy wrap itself around my ankles. I lifted my leg, straining against the bindings, but they held on tight. I watched in fascinated horror as tendrils coiled up my legs like living snakes, entwining my body in a constricting prison.

"Help, Love! Help!"

I struggled, straining against my self-inflicted bars of a many-faceted analysis.

"You are created, fearfully and wonderfully."

"Yes, but so much is rubbish and needs transforming," I squealed, wriggling.

"And yet you cannot change even a hair of your head."

I fought against the tightening grip of the net I had woven, and entangled myself further within my self-judgments. The thick stem of self-creation wound its way around my decision to change and be more like God.

"Help," I squeaked again.

"Trust the work to Me."

He directed my focus inward. I cringed at the masks of insecurity and fear that lurked in my depths. Shutting my eyes, I held onto the love I knew was in His heart for me.

"Look."

I peered through slitted eyes, and there, in the central core of my being was a spark, flickering like a star in a dark velvet sky. Jewelled light flashed from it in a waterfall of colour that washed through me.

"Wow, what is that?"

"It is a piece of Me. Everyone I breathe life into carries My Image."

Amazing! I have a God particle!

᪣ *CHARMS* ᪣

"Right."

I bounded out of bed. With military precision and a very straight back, I washed, dressed, breakfasted and summoned resolve. Today I was going to dedicate wholly to prayer. Prayer for all those I wanted Him to introduce Himself to. I shook out my mental shopping list and found a place undisturbed by the world. And I was off, jumping every hurdle like a well-trained racehorse. Choosing my words carefully, I entreated, implored and even whined with the firm belief I would be answered. Determined in my convictions, I gave Him no rest. I stormed the gates with undeniable fervour. At intervals I would take myself off to a watering hole and renew my vigour in order to be able to continue my assailment of the heavens.

"Phew," I expelled after several hours of dogged endurance and insatiable requests.

A rather effective day, although I say it myself, I thought smugly.

Somewhere in the room I sensed His presence, and there it was; the eyebrow was up!

"Hmm." I stood, hands on hips and sassed as effectively as any teenager. He watched me, a slight frown creasing His brow. Uncertainty wriggled in the pit of my stomach.

"Tell Me, beloved, where did you learn to demand so fervently?"

Uh-oh.

He did not require an answer.

"Did you seek My presence?"

No...

"Did you seek My will?"

No...

Sudden indignation produced an ugly self-righteous slither.

"But I did pray in Your Name, so You are duty-bound to answer!"

Intense silence like thick fog descended on me. The fog became the pillar of cloud. Within the cloud was the Glory, the Majesty and the Might of He Who created all and knows all. I lifted my arms to shield my closed eyelids from the burning illumination. There I remained, unable to move, held rigid by Holy Fear. Encircled increasingly by the One I belonged to.

"Forgive me my King," I implored in less than a whisper.

Fire covered me and I felt the dross of self-righteous arrogance rise to the surface, and sharp-yet-sweet pain when His hand cleansed it from me. The cloud lifted. I dared to look up. His hand extended. Taking it, I rose to stand beside Him.

"You cannot add My Name to your prayer like a charm and expect Me to perform. My Name is Who I AM. When you pray from a place of the fullness of I AM, then you pray in My Name."

All my praying was silent.

❧ *UNLOVED* ❧

Leaves rustled in close companionship as we moved through the tunnel of green. Intermittent rays of dazzling sunlight glinted between the foliage. Blinking in the brilliance, I beamed at Him.

"It is good to be alive on a morning such as this."

"It is good to be alive. Yes," His words caused ripples of implication that reached my core. We paused and He directed my vision to a large cherry tree growing near the path. Rich ruby fruit dangled enticingly just out of reach. He pulled down a branch laden with gleaming baubles for me to pick a handful.

"Thank you!" I exclaimed with delight.

Biting into the ripe fruit, the skin popped satisfyingly and juice filled my mouth. I was surprised by the lack of flavour. The colour, the form, everything was perfect except the taste.

Perhaps it's me.

I continued to munch through the handful, ever hopeful of a sweet encounter but disappointed, until my hand was empty. His eyes searched me and I was held captive in His gaze. He released me and we continued to walk.

What was that all about?

He offered no explanation.

Patience. He will tell me when He is ready.

"Maybe it is when you are ready."

I can't get away with anything!

A cool breeze blew the rich smells of ripening growth all around us. We inhaled deeply in unison. Again He stopped and turned me towards another cherry. This was an altogether different tree. The cherries were a pale yellow touched with a pink blush. They looked unpalatable and a little insipid. I raised an eyebrow at Him.

"Try one," He said picking a single cherry and placing it in my open hand.

Its skin was smooth and taut as I squeezed slightly. Popping it in my mouth without expectation, I bit down and the cherry exploded with juice. Warmth and sweetness filled my mouth like heavenly nectar. The delectable and unique flavour of perfectly ripe fruit saturated my senses.

"Wow!" I exclaimed in surprise.

"Yes, some have all the external appearance, but others have the internal reality."

My mind was transported back to a scene earlier in my walk.

In the centre of a long hall, a number of animated dogs surrounded a small confused puppy. Each dog was barking and yelping its own peculiar argument of instruction at the unloved one cringing in their midst. The effect was a deafening barrage of aggression. The puppy cowered, the fur along its back rising in a ridge of fearful reaction. Silently the door at the end of the hall swung inward, revealing a young bitch, sitting with her head on one side as though listening. She raised her head and padded, slowly and purposefully, towards the alpha male. Touching noses, she nudged him aside. All eyes fixed on her in an electric silence. She looked only at the puppy. Sitting in the place of the alpha, she began to sing. A song of love from one heart to another. A song to woo all the depths of the unloved. I swayed with the tender wave upon wave of crooning music, tears prickling the backs of my eyes. The puppy's hackles sank back into fluff, and after shaking away the remains of distress, it plodded to the bitch, gazed at her adoringly and sat down between her front paws.

Tenderness flooded me with the satisfaction of a happy ending.

Later, when the day was moving into the realm of memory, I settled into His presence and listened.

"It is through the heart, not through argument, that you will reach those who believe they are unloved. And only those with the internal reality know the song."

✥ STAFF ✥

"Come," the call insisted, rousing me from restless sleep.

It's still dark.

"Come," the call came again. Heavy authority filled the room.

Come where?

I responded hesitantly. The night was pitch. The sounds of my uncertain stumbling were swallowed by darkness as I staggered in His direction. The call drew me far into the hills along unfamiliar paths. At last I saw Him, a shifting light against the deep sky. The Shepherd of my soul.

He stood tall and commanding, His robe billowing, His curved staff upright. I scurried eagerly up the embankment. He spun around and set off at a pace I could not hope to match. I pursued Him, rocks jabbing at my feet, casting me down again and again. Determined in my pain, I ran bleeding, sobs catching in my throat.

"Wait, please wait."

Nothing.

Why doesn't He wait?

He disappeared over the brow of the hill. I blundered blindly, the heaviness pressing my lungs into suffocation. I had to find Him. I did not know the way back. Or the way forward. I was lost in the dark. Alone. The piercing screech of an owl ripped through the cold air. I clutched at tufts of grass as I pulled myself up the steep bank. Something rustled in a patch of dense shadow. I held my breath. A streak of living lightning shot across the night. He leaped into the gloom, His staff spinning over His head. A small bundle of limbs whirled up and around, caught in the hook. He took hold of it and strode towards me, thrusting the leggy softness into my arms. I stared aghast at the tiny fawn. The new day filtered over the horizon, bathing us in shafts of clear light. I looked down at the small creature. Its head lolled against me, bruised from His staff.

"You hurt it!" I stated indignantly.

He looked at me and my knees buckled, trembling. His face reflected sharp light, and His eyes burned into my soul. I dropped to the ground.

Who is this fearful Shepherd? I hardly recognise Him.

"Look at Me."

His face flashed so fiercely I could hardly bear it. Power radiated from Him in unending surges. I lay unable to move or breathe. The fawn was as still as death beside me. Gradually the brilliance faded, and I saw the Love behind the power. Taking deep draughts of air and clutching the shuddering fawn, I dared to search Him for understanding.

"Come."

He led me to the shadow, where the incident had taken place. The risen sun revealed all. I stared in horror. The ground fell away in a hidden ravine. Sharp rocks, like jagged teeth, disappeared into mist far beneath us. I stepped back from the edge, my head whirling.

He was saving its life!

I offered the trembling creature. He took it gently and lifted it onto one shoulder. We walked together into the dawn; He, complete as ever, me, a little wiser.

∾ SEALED ∾

The birds outside my open window trilled with anticipation, waking me. Stretching out of bed, I jiggled with excitement.

Wow! Is that for me?

Leaning against the door frame was the cause of the excitement. A long wooden staff with a top end that curved.

It's just like His.

I hopped about, climbing into a variety of clothes, all the while grinning at the staff standing tall and straight by the door.

"Ready?"

The call of my Shepherd churned excitement into frenzy.

"Yes, yes, YES!" I squealed.

My hand closed around the smooth wood. Authority tingled up my arm and flowed throughout my body.

The back door banged behind me, and my feet found the cold grass leading up to the place of meeting. He was waiting, His own staff in hand. Light played on His hair, creating a haze of halo, and all else faded beside Him.

"Well done." His tone held all the sacrifices I had made in the days gone by. I basked in His praise.

"Onward," He declared and with a jump He started off at a good pace across the plain and out into the rugged fells beyond.

"Wait for me!" I yelled, slipping and sliding behind him, my staff dragging uselessly along the ground.

"Use your staff," He commanded.

I watched as He planted His firmly before taking a step.

Hmm, that doesn't look so hard.

I fumbled and tumbled after Him, muttering under my breath. I could hear the faintest hint of laughter. Looking up, I caught Him watching me, His face a picture of humour. I giggled, and He moved more slowly, leading me and teaching me how to use my new staff.

We stopped at regular intervals to gather stray sheep. They trotted along behind us, following in a growing group. Once, He leaned over a wall and lifted a rather ample ewe back onto our side. I watched her shake vigorously and turn back to the wall whereupon He caught her around the neck with the curve of the crook and gently but firmly led her alongside us until she walked without pulling. Eventually He let her go and she joined the group, but I noticed He often cast an eye in her direction. At one time there were three tired lambs in His arms, all on top of each other and slipping in and out of sleep. He held them close and tight until they revived, at which point they began to fidget, and He put them down with a smile and a pat.

He stopped at a circular yard, enclosed by a grey stone wall covered with little cushions of soft green moss. Opening the gate, He guided the sheep through. I was allowed to collect the strays and lead them in, using my staff to gently guide them. However, the particularly difficult and ample ewe gave me such a shove that I fell back into a foul smelling ditch.

"Oi!" I shouted indignantly, digging mud out of one ear.

"Be firm," He ordered.

Be firm! I'll give her what for if I get hold of her!

I charged in, jabbing the ewe from behind. She veered off bleating and came around the back of me, her head down in a butting charge. I brandished my staff at the ready.

"Watch."

He took some coarse grass from between the rocks and walked to the ewe. Allowing her to sniff the grass, He then turned and walked into the enclosure. She, of course, followed like a lamb. I bristled.

"It is more effective to lead from the front than to drive from behind."

Once all the flock were enclosed, I went in after them. Half-way around the wall was a gated alley of stone, leading through a narrowed opening, to another identical enclosure. From above they would have looked like spectacles without arms.

"I want you to lead them through." He looked at me with a gleam in His eye.

What is He up to?

He opened the gate to the second yard, I led the sheep and lambs through the alley towards Him, using grass to encourage and the hook to guide. They came cautiously and were rewarded with a mouthful of greenery. As they reached Him, He held them for a moment, then let them out into the second enclosure. I stretched to see what He was doing.

"Bring the last one all the way."

And guess who? Yep, the awkward ewe! She came. She stopped. She started. She stopped and stared. She tried to turn but the alley was too narrow. I patted her face and held the grass under her nose. She eyed me doubtfully and walked slowly along behind me.

If she butts me again, I'm going to smack her!

Love's hands reached for her and she surrendered. He lifted her onto His lap and, placing His hands on her head, He gave her His blessing. Then taking an ear, He clipped her with an ear-ring, and she bounded off to join the others. I looked at Him with my eyebrows up. He looked back with shining eyes.

"All those that are Mine bear My seal. Even the awkward ones!"

Hrmph! Feeling a little squirmy!

∽ *MOTHS* ∾

It felt good to be out of the cold and back in my comfortable house. I snuggled into the softness of the armchair and pulled a fleece blanket around my shoulders. A quiet flick and flutter caught my attention, and I noticed several moths knocking on the window pane.

"Open the window."

His voice sounded internally, gaining momentum until I reached up and lifted the latch. With a click the window swung open. The evening's damp fingers groped their way into the room followed by two light-hungry moths.

I shut the window and retreated into my blanket to watch. One of the moths flew straight into the flickering candle burning on the table and was instantly and utterly consumed. The other flew haphazardly at the flickering flame, almost touching but never quite. Then, exhausted by the race, it expired on the floor at my feet.

I wonder what He's getting at...

I dozed off.

Images from the past dreamed their way through my consciousness. A few friends sitting comfortably together in a sparsely furnished room. The ding-dong of the doorbell interrupted their communal prayers. On the threshold stood a young woman with a wild countenance, nervously twisting her fingers around each other.

"I'm, I'm s-s-sorry to ring your b-b-bell," she stuttered, confusion wrapped around every word.

"I-I-I don't really know, why I-I-I'm here, but every time I leave my house, I-I find myself at your door." Her shoulders sagged with the relief of discharged struggle.

My heart ached with longing as I looked at her through His eyes. She hungered for a food she didn't know existed. I opened the door wide and invited her to join us. She stepped over the threshold hesitantly and looked around, caution and hope written in her features. Before the door closed, another arrived. A large man in a leather studded jacket stepped through the opening. He eyed me with a fearful frown and moved to the other side of the room, where he slunk back against the wall. Settling into the contemplative circle, my friends continued their focus and prayers to the Light of the world. The wild one leaned forward, and with her eyes wide open, she stepped nearer. As the mystery of recognition took place, her face flickered with reflected light. Eagerly she flew to the centre. I watched in silent joy as His presence enveloped and consumed her completely. The fear-shrouded man shrank to the floor, shaking within his studded-leather prison.

Warm breath on my face and I woke.

"Love?" I yawned.

The embrace of Love surpassed all the cosy blankets in all the world.

"Those who hunger for light will be drawn to Me through those who shine."

❧ *TREES* ❧

The limbs of the forest snatched at my hair with clasping gnarly fingers. The dark-green canopy above, weighed on my shoulders with increasing melancholy. I dragged myself heavily through the undergrowth. The squawks and flaps of disturbed birds fled into the distance. I slapped each trunk as I passed, flattening my hands against the rough bark and pushing myself from tree to tree. I searched for any glimmer of high ground in desperate defeat. At last my feet turned their toes upward, and a slight and welcome rise lifted each step. I drew in a breath of leaf mould, coating my lungs with a damp, earthy mist.

Where am I?

The top of the hill wore a dense cloak of black poplar and horse chestnut. My groans drowned the singing of the quivering leaves.

I'm gonna have to climb one of these giants!

I approached a low branched chestnut and, grunting, began the arduous hand-over-foot ascent, up through the criss-cross of boughs, to the swaying tops. Through a face full of leaves, I burst through to blue sky. Slowly turning, I surveyed the puffy tops, scrutinizing the landscape for anything hopeful. Nothing but endless shades of green. My spirit sank with my descent. At the bottom, I remembered Him.

"Love, help me! This forest is vast and I am lost."

"You are never lost when you are with Me!"

"But I don't know where I am."

"That is not the same as being lost."

I am tired and I want to be home.

"Please just tell me where I am supposed to go without the cryptic puzzle!"

"Stay where you are and look around you. Tell Me what do you see?"

Here we go.

"I see trees, trees and more trees!" I shifted from one aching foot to the other.

Silence.

"OK, I see slender birches, their tops touching in the breeze. I see stately oaks growing saplings in their shade. I see the ground soft with a carpet of last year's leaves. I see birds sheltering in groups. I see tiny trees and I see enormous trees. I see wobbly bushes and gnarly roots. The dark fans of pines. Shining spikey hollies. Silver leaved limes and steady horse chestnuts. This forest has every tree!"

I waited hopefully.

"I will tell you what I see."

I sat down in the roots of a poplar. The soft earth gave way as I shuffled and wriggled into a listening position.

"I see thousands upon thousands of individual lives. I see each one in its entirety, from its outer form to its inner spark. Every life's story is laid out plainly before Me. Nothing escapes My eye. For every life, without preference, I provide light and water and I watch all grow. Everyone is unique in their growth and nature. I AM full of the knowledge of all and I AM filled with love for all."

I strolled home with Him in thoughtful praise.

∽ *LOVED* ∾

"Let's talk about Love."

"Ok." I hesitated, sensing something more behind His words.

"Whom do you love?"

"You." I answered simply.

We stood on the bridge, looking over together at the busy streets below us. Bodies melted into one as the hundreds jostled their way through each other and onward into separate lives. They all wore masks of glassy-eyed indifference.

"And them?"

"Are You are talking about loving You with all that I am and loving others as I love myself?" I questioned hesitantly.

"Yes." His voice was smiling.

A large sigh fell over the side of the bridge.

"It is hard. You are easy to love, but them…" I gestured in the direction of my sigh.

"How is it possible when they are so unlovable, and half the time they don't even want to be loved?"

"Why do you love Me?"

I took a step back from the edge. Utter acceptance and overwhelming love flowed from Him until I burned with the knowledge and gratitude of His great love for me.

"I love You because You love me and I can't help but love You back."

"Yes." Love and light radiated.

"And then?"

I felt the power of His love rush through my veins like fire, my heart blazed and I loved all without exception or partiality. Inner light dawned.

"And then, I love with Your love."

"And is love diminished if the beloved is unlovely?"

"It is not," I gasped.

"And is love diminished if the beloved refuses to be loved?"

I found my heart breaking with the beloved's rejection of His love, not from the place of self but from the place of knowing the beloved's need.

"It is not quenched but it hurts."

His mantle enveloped me and we revelled in love's completeness.

❧ *KEY* ❧

I stared at the shape of the cross in the palm of my hand, its cool metal clean-cut and flat against my skin.

"What is it, Love?"

A shift in focus and He was there. I looked at Him looking at me. I could see my face reflected in miniature in His eyes. His eyes, with their warmth and depth. A flush of exhilaration rose in my chest, and I felt the urge to throw my arms around Him. He laughed, a deep resonating roar that shook the ground. His overalls sprayed flakes of dried clay over me.

What is He wearing!

"Come. I have something to show you."

We entered a large shed lit by a clear white light. In its centre was a long table covered in models of all shapes and sizes. The dusty smell of drying clay filled the room. I watched fascinated as He picked up a lump, and moulded and carved intricate shapes and patterns into it. Cocooning His hands, He folded an outer skin around it, and I gasped in recognition at the shape that slowly formed. It was me.

"I made you exactly how I wanted you. All your gifts and talents come from Me."

His eyes with their deep knowing delved into depths I was blind to.

I thought about my childhood, how I had excelled at some things, even before I knew Him. I had used them to my own advantage, but they had not satisfied. I had developed my own gifts in a way that had excluded the Giver.

How strange that I have never seen this before.

He held out His hand, and I looked at Him uncomprehending.

"The key."

Ah, it's a key!

Now for the first time I noticed my clay counterpart had a cavity in its centre. The key fitted perfectly, and as He turned it, I saw the well of unlimited life unlock. Living water gurgled and churned within my soul, infusing every part, every gift and talent. Enhancing the God-made talents and slotting them perfectly into their positions. Completing them with the living wisdom of the One Who knew what they were for and how to use them.

"Every perfect gift takes its perfect place when known in relation to Me."

I am blessed.

✶ CREATION ✷

The sky lit up with pink and orange reflections. I gazed in awe at the colours of the sunrise from the brow of the hill, halfway around my morning walk.

If I painted it, no one would believe it was real.

A delicious breeze stirred my heart, revealing His presence. We stood together and watched His beauty unfold.

"This land is truly blessed, Love."

His peace stilled me and holy fear claimed the space within. Something was coming, a heavy lesson. The air turned thick with expectancy, and darkness wrapped itself around us like a cloak. I clung to Him. Strength and determination passed into me.

Sudden shafts of dazzling rays cut through the velvet blackness, shredding the dark like paper. In the centre of the light was a man and a woman. Their heads were bowed with sorrow. A thousand broken-hearted angels wept over them, their tears falling like rain.

My eyes stung and my airways clogged.

"What has happened?"

"These are Father's first created children."

Steeling my resolve, I focussed on the scene before us. The couple moved slowly together, dragging their feet away from the lighted ground. They entered the gloom, and I could no longer see them.

"What? Where?" I asked.

"Keep watching."

I waited. Slowly a dismal day began to dawn, and a sin-sick sun dragged itself out of a sea of ink. It revealed a land of emerging malevolence. A harsh land convulsing with disease. A dying land clawing at life with rotting limbs.

"The land is cursed," I whispered in shock.

My heart ached with sadness as I witnessed innocence and beauty mutate, into vileness and perversion. The sorrow of the angels entered my soul, and I wept on His shoulder. His own tears splashed hot on my head as He held my face to the world.

"Keep watching," He repeated.

Before me was the tree on which He reclaimed Father's creation. The law of sin's wages hung on scales in the heavens above Him. The law that secured the death of evil and the eternity of good. Darkness embraced all. Light awaited its perfect moment. A drop of blood fell, swelling to become a vast ocean that flowed in everlasting purity. The King of all creation awoke and arose victorious.

"You have broken the curse on the land!" Joy broke from me in choking sobs.

"Yes."

There was more, there is always more.

The couple lay prostrate before Him. The drop of blood splashed, soaking, saturating all their unclean ugliness and transforming it into pure beauty.

My face lifted in elation, dried tears crinkled the skin on my cheeks.

"This is wonderful to me, my Love. You are wonderful to me."

He has given us His all, and without Him there is no redemption.

"Innocence can be marred and is the babe of creation. Purity cannot and is the maturity of creation."

"Thank you, my own Saviour."

✦ *WIND* ✦

I looked out over the land; the rich artistry of the season's colours looked back. Aged trees clothed in autumn, stood tall beside me. The wind picked up, its seeking fingers pulling at my jacket, for a way in. I scrunched my arms around myself and pulled my coat tighter.

"Beloved."

Ah, there He is.

"Love." I absorbed His presence.

A hush crept over me, and the wind lulled into stillness. The world took a deep breath. The aged ones felt it first. The gentle murmur of leaves in conversation escalated to swishing, and shadow shimmered into light as they trembled and spun. The movement grew in tempo, until they were singing at fever pitch in exultation at being swept into the air by a force so powerful there is no resistance, only surrender.

I was safe in His arms. Immovable unless He willed it. My hair whipped around my face. Boughs rocked in clacking rhythm until even their trunks were dancing with the song. Gold and red clusters swirled their whirlwind tornadoes about us and finally flew freely into the distance.

"The wind blows where it will, and although invisible to your eyes, you can see its effect and feel its power."

I surged with the desire to run and leap into this wild wind. To dance with the leaves and sing the song of creation in its eternal celebration.

His laughter rang out, and in surprise I saw that He too desired to run with the wind.

Even now, I know so little of Him.

❧ *ENERGY* ❧

Clouds drifted across an azure sky. The sun's
golden rays drenched the land, illuminating the
world. A sun-bow shone orange and green in a
partial arc through a gap in the grey. Seagulls
dipped and dived into the earth-rich field,
scavenging for food, their wings flashing like
white sails on a windswept ocean. A sudden crack
as a shot was fired, shattering the reverie with its
shocking violence. A gull dropped from its lofty
existence and thumped onto the dark soil. I
watched, pain streaking through me like a hot
knife. The desire to help rushed through my soul.
I looked into the face of Love.

"Wait."

I fidgeted a whole waiting minute before speeding off towards the injured bird. The mud stuck to my boots and the wind fought against me. Leaning forward, I soldiered on, determined in my mission of rescue. Puffing, I knelt beside the twitching creature and painstakingly checked for damage. Wing feathers and bone hung uselessly by a silken thread. This bird would never soar the ocean skies again.

"What do I do?" My words caught in my throat like barbed wire.

Tightness in my chest threatened to heave up and spill from my eyes. The bird began to thrash, feathers flying, squawking. Its death throes clutching at me in fear.

"Help him!" I wailed desperately.

"Why are you here?" His still voice crept through my crashing helplessness.

"I, I came to help," I stuttered.

I don't understand. Love needs to help.

"Yes, Love's very nature is to help".

"So help it!" I almost shouted.

"Do you know the nature of Love's help?"

Please don't give me a lesson now.

"Please, please, this poor animal is suffering," my voice wilted.

"Suffering is part of the all of Love. It is an instrument Love uses to reach the depths. An instrument it uses to bring union with its beloved."

This feels so cruel. I cannot watch any more.

I dissolved in the mud and ached with pain for the bird, as the shuddering subsided and the creature lay still. Absently I stroked the soft feathers of the discarded body. Numbness crept its way into my bones. Broken inside, I went home. Later I approached Him Whom my heart loves.

"Why? Why did You do nothing?"

Through His eyes I saw the dark earth of the field and my blundering helplessness, despite His word to wait. Drawing the vision back from the field, I caught a fleeting glimpse of a hare caught in a thicket, struggling to free itself. As I'd stumbled my way towards my own desire, He'd reached forth His hand and opened the thicket to free the hare from its prickly prison. At the same time the hand of Father had come down from heaven and drawn the dying gull out from within its suffering. Understanding opened the narrow door of judgment within me. I had sought to help that which only Father could, and in doing so had missed my purpose. Failure wrapped its ugly noose around my neck. Hanging my head in shame, I looked away from Him Who loves me.

Forgive me, I could not speak it.

"Of course," compassion filled His words, but my head would not rise.

"I cannot face You," I choked.

"All things are in My hands. Your help is not just for the good of others; it is also to bring you closer to Me and My Way."

He lifted my head. His face shone with such tenderness my shame was undone and my heart was healed.

"Teach me as You love me," I gazed up at Him.

"Do not use your energy where I do not send you. You will need it where I do."

❧ GROWTH ❧

The early morning washed the landscape with its brand new palette. The path we trod was lined with hedgerow; leaves waved at us with the caress of a light breeze as we passed. The scent of dew was released freshly with every step onto the fresh green carpet beneath our feet. Turning off the path, He led me up a slope which increased in gradient as we went. I felt His face centring on mine, and I waited for His word.

"Do you remember this mountain?"

I was transported back to a climb very different from this one. Dark storm clouds covered the ragged mountain top, wrapping their cloying mist around me, leading me this way and that. Freezing rain beat mercilessly at my face like hundreds of stinging needles. Untamed wind whipped me, tugging at my clothes and chilling my bones. My legs, like wooden blocks, resolute in their ascent, stomped slowly up the frozen track. Ankles turning, breath grasping, eyes squeezed shut and face turned away.

"Yes, I remember."

It seems so very different this time.

"The mountain is the same, it is you who are different."

"Yes," I wondered. "I am different."

Looking up at the mountain, what had once been a formidable height, now presented as an inviting adventure. I stood a little straighter. The ascension of the incline was hardly noticeable. I pondered Him, following His steps closely. My own footprints fitted easily into His impressions in the softened mud. As we conquered the top, I found that I had arrived, with minimal effort.

How can it be that I am so different?

"You have been walking with Me for some time now. You have become accustomed to aligning yourself with My Way. And you have gained strength in your growth."

How amazing, I had hardly noticed it happening!

⨴ *ALL* ⨵

We stood at the top of the mountain, united both in climb and love. His words fell upon me like fresh bread, feeding my soul.

"I AM all-present."

Then Father was there with the Beautiful Spirit, spreading inward and outward, extending abundantly throughout the world I could see and beyond to the world I couldn't. There was no upturned stone They were not already under. Every nook, every cranny, They preceded my sight and continued on long past its farthest reach. Turning inward, I saw They went to the very heart of me; my core lurched, and I found

They went deeper than I knew I was. They were everywhere completely. I settled in trust with the assurance of Their all-encompassing love that left nowhere untouched.

"I AM all-knowing."

The voice directed my thoughts. My mind was opened, and I glimpsed the totality of Their knowledge. How They knew all my beginnings before I began. How Their knowing stretched into all my 'nows' of the present and the future, even beyond the grave. My mind boggled with the knowledge that filled The Three. Nowhere, nothing, no one and no-when was unknown to Them.

"I AM all-power."

The words leapt in me; my knees shook and the hair on the back of my neck stood on end. Streams of light pierced the ground at our feet. The mountain rumbled and shook at its roots. The earth fell away in great mouthfuls to crash down undigested into the sea. A roar and the sea fled, leaving its bed naked and exposed. A crack and the earth split; from the opening there came creatures of such magnitude that they dwarfed the mountain and the light of the sun was blocked by their wings. They circled us and the wind from their wings was like a hurricane. Their eyes flashed with fire and their breath burned the air from my lungs. My heart stopped. I staggered to hide behind my Saviour.

They spoke a word I did not understand, and I watched from my safe place, awestruck as the great creatures bowed their massive heads before The Three. I saw a glimpse of the edge of Their power. A power so great that my wildest dreams were a drop of water in a universe of oceans.

"My all-ness grows eternally. There is no before Me and no after Me. I AM always and forever. My creation will never outgrow Me."

I slept, exhausted.

✎ LONGING ✐

It rained heavily last night.

Love surveyed His creation from a-far. Olive-green fields with mottled hedges lay sleeping. Rusty leaves clung in crackled bunches, starkly outlined against the clear blue. A pair of doves, wings flashing with reflected sunlight, flew overhead where the sky deepened to royalty. On the horizon the hazy line of grey sea melted into the almost white of the distance. A few late trees burned with autumn golds, and soft jade moss blanketed their bare bark. A spattering of yellow lit up intermittently as solitary leaves on sparsely clad bushes quivered with little whips of wind. At their roots, puddled mirrors of light splashed and blades of mud-coated grass trembled. The last rosy-tinted fruits wavered invitingly above. His arm reached high and brought down a branch. Plucking several, I filled my pockets to take home. Choosing one, I savoured the smooth skin before crunching into the crisp coldness.

"Mmmm, Your world is beautiful."

His expression held an ache of such longing that the apple turned to dust in my mouth and I gagged. With a dull thud, the unfinished fruit landed at my feet. Bending, He picked it up and, wiping it clean, returned it to my hand. Its wet skin seeped into my skin. I shivered.

Something is wrong.

The apple forgotten, I studied Him. The King of the world.

"Look again," His gentle tone was almost unbearable, and a great sorrow touched my heart.

When I looked, we were sitting on a bench in the middle of bustling city life. Everywhere, people jostled, squashing themselves into every space and squeezing through impassable gaps. A multitude of individualities passed before our viewpoint.

I watched a watcher. He leered over his prey like a waiting vulture. Taking a brave breath, I questioned Love with an eyebrow.

"He searches to fill the void he carries."

A group of shivering women slunk in darkened doorways, agonisingly enticing in their painted masks of entrapment. I looked to Him again for understanding.

"They searched for love in the wrong place and were taken captive."

I jumped as a shining red car raced by, almost climbing the pavement, followed nose to boot by a sleek black number with silver wheels. They disappeared around a bend in the road leaving their roaring engines ringing in my ears. Love's voice cut softly through my jangled nerves.

"My Father's children use many things to try to fill the deep emptiness they feel; they rush from one distraction on to the next in quick succession, for fear that if they stand still they will find there is nothing more than the hollow lives they have built around themselves."

An old woman in a coat that dripped with rags shuffled unseeing onto the seat beside me. She fumbled with one of the many bags attached to her arms. A sharp intake of breath, and in my release a moan escaped.

"Yes, she is despair; she has believed the lie that there is nothing more than she can see with her own eyes."

My face threatened to cave in. I swallowed a great gulp of grief and stared agonisingly at the wretched faces all around me. Eyes like deep caverns, haunted by evil. Hearts devoured by fear and anger. Those wearing abuse like a defining garment. Parents' bowed down in isolated responsibility over their little treasures with no knowledge of the Great Parent Who loves them all. The created, moving in all directions, searching, but never finding their way home. Polluted air mingled with exhaled smoke drifted over me. I coughed, suffocating in the multitude of suffering souls surrounding me, clamouring in their anguish for a glimmer of hope. Desolation threatened to overwhelm the world. I reached for Him. His face was wet with the tears I had suppressed. His heart's desire gushed in an unending flood of longing, and I knew the yearning heart of Love. Silence descended like a blanket of snow over the world, and Love's voice rang out.

"I will go."

I sat up startled; His words entered all creation and, through my tears, golden rays penetrated the darkest despair and illuminated His world.

Hope was born and Love took His place. I gazed up at Him with tears of a different hue wetting my cheeks. Father embraced Son. Love held out a bleeding hand to me, and I joined Him.

"My Father's children ran away once, and now they are lost in their disobedience. But I have made a Way and I AM come to bring them home."

Joy exploded from Father's heart, and we sang the song of salvation to the hills.

❧ *CLEAN* ❧

I regulated my breathing as we ascended. Half-way up, a combination of beech and oak began to rise alongside our path, beginning in gathered stumps and growing taller as we walked. At the summit, the world opened into a sunlit sky freckled with flitting birds, carrying tiny sticks to adorn their next home. Then began the descent. Pines intruded, crowding the light and dense gloom clouded my eyes. Down, down, down, into the darkest dell we journeyed. Nothing stirred. Silent desolation dominated even though I walked beside Him. I jumped at the sudden snap of a trodden twig. Someone else was in the wood. I glanced nervously at my Companion. He strode upright ever onward. Through the pillar-like trunks I spied another traveller. He moved fast, and on his approach my skin bristled with unease.

Who is he? What is he doing here?

The stranger's face, a mask of false compassion, leaned eagerly toward me as he reached out and touched my arm. I recoiled as slivers of confusion stabbed at my mind.

"No," I stated simply and firmly.

Weight issued from my word, delivering me from his darkness as he departed. I looked up at my Companion, still He marched, and nothing veered Him from His path.

Up we trudged, to claim the highest ground. My boots heavy with mud, I wheezed my way one single-minded step after another. The birds chirped encouragement, and aligning my will with His, I claimed the strength that drove me forward. The world's muck clung to my boots, climbing, sliming up and over their tops, clasping, grasping at my socks, then creeping, seeping through to touch my skin with cold and clammy filth.

I reached the top in exhausted victory. He took my hands, and leading me to a stile, He bade me sit. The world became soundless as He knelt at my feet.

"What are You doing?" I rasped in breathless bewilderment.

In His lap appeared a bowl of crystal water. With His hands He removed my mud caked boots and socks.

"But..," I spluttered, humiliated and ashamed.

His eyes sought me, and in them was the authority of the King. His hands, firm yet gentle, found out all the dirt and washed me until it was gone and I was clean. I bowed my head in humble gratitude, my feet tingling with the cool air as He dried them.

The birds sang songs of praise. I walked on air all the way home, and the ground never touched my feet.

⋖ *HOLD ME* ⋗

Sitting quietly in the early morning, the world outside still sleeping, I waited for Him. I was rewarded in my waiting, and time flowed into eternity.

"Hold Me," His voice was heavy with intent.

What... Why...?

"My Love, Your voice, it is full of such meaning and depth, and yet... I cannot find the words. Are You in pain?"

Silence so loud I covered my ears. My heart thudded towards Him. My words fell over each other in their attempt to discover Him.

"Is this great passion Your desire for me? Is it me? Have I done something to hurt You?"

"You have not."

The inner Presence grew so deep I was overcome, and I cried out.

"What is it, Love? What can I do?"

"Hold Me."

"I don't know how," I whispered to the great desire.

I am not enough to hold Him, yet if He asks it of me, I will do all I can.

"I will hold You until forever and beyond. I will hold You in the deepest places, in the darkest places. I will hold You with all that I am and embrace all that You are."

My arms wrapped around Him, and I kissed the life He gave me back into Him. Hesitant for a moment as to what it might mean for me but then determined in my love for Him. And in that moment at least, I knew that I truly loved Him, more than I loved myself.

❧ *FUSION* ❧

"Fusion."

The word echoed momentously within my spirit. Fumbling with the dictionary in eager knowledge of something revelatory, I read:

'Fusion: The joining together of two nuclei. The process of causing two components to melt together with intense heat so that there is no separate individuality but a whole new substance is created.'

But I am unclean. I withdrew an inner step.

"How can You? I know what is in me, I am flawed."

I felt no shame, just brutal honesty at my own imperfections. My heart wrenched in spasms of incomprehension at His desire to unite Himself with me in totality.

"It is in absolute fusion that I AM able to absorb all your depths of impurity and so absolve them completely."

Falling to my knees, I cried out:

"Oh my Saviour and my God!"

The truth of Him fused with my inner being in utter wholeness. Blending, melting together with heat born of holiness. I was re-formed and made new. I, became we, became I am. The two became one, and I was re-created into an image of God.

✍ *HIS GARDEN* ➣

Aware though asleep, I listened to the newness of sound from my place of recent revelation. The world outside moved through its created motions in a circle of temporary learning. The world inside was aglow with glory. I moved slowly in my garden. The ivory silk of my dress floated gracefully over the vibrantly growing meadow. Flowers spun their seeds in twirls of crimson and gold. Butterflies took flight on delicate wings of rainbow lace. The touch of grass under my bare feet was as soft as fur. He was waiting. His face shone with magnificent beauty, so far beyond description that my heart leapt and I ran into His open arms. His love surrounded me and I discovered...

There is a Garden within Him!

꩜ *THE BEGINNING* ꩜

TITLES IN THIS SERIES

❧ THE GARDEN ☙

❧ THE GARDEN BEYOND ☙

❧ THE GARDEN WITHIN ☙

Copies available from
www.christart.co.uk
www.amazon.co.uk
www.eden.co.uk

CPSIA information can be obtained
at www.ICGtesting.com
Printed in the USA
LVOW13s2215100118
562549LV00015B/1400/P